THE
STRANGLERS

Then & Now

In memory of
Dave Greenfield
1949 - 2020

THE
STRANGLERS

Then & Now

WYMER
PUBLISHING
Bedford, England

First published in Great Britain in 2018
by Wymer Publishing
www.wymerpublishing.co.uk
Tel: 01234 326691
Wymer Publishing is a trading name of Wymer (UK) Ltd

ISBN: 978-1-912782-88-8

Typeset by The Andys.
Printed and bound in England by Harrier LLC.

A catalogue record for this book is available from the British Library.

Cover design by The Andys.
Front cover photo © Steve Emberton

INTRODUCTION

No matter how much some might protest, bands invariably get labelled within a specific genre. No, don't worry, I'm not even going to mention the word! But there is no escaping the fact that the late seventies saw a sea change within the world of rock music and for good or for bad The Stranglers just happened to be one of those bands in the right place at the right time.

So even though I am sticking to my promise and not mentioning the word, for the most part, there was a far more aggressive approach to the music from a majority of the bands that emerged around '76-77. None more so than The Stranglers. Also in keeping with the atmosphere, The Stranglers didn't exactly go out of their way to endear themselves to the journalists and the media — that conventional wisdom said you needed on your side if you wanted to succeed in the murky world of the music business.

The Stranglers appeared to ignore such wisdom. Did it do them any harm? It could be argued they might have become a bigger band. It could be argued that they often cut off their own noses to spite their faces, but the one defining thing that shines through is that The Stranglers have always stuck to their principles.

And the reason why I still won't use that word? It often proved to be a millstone around the necks of so many young bands that burst on to the scene during those chaotic years of the late seventies. No sooner were they up and running, many of those bands fell by the wayside and were gone again within a couple of years or so.

Not so The Stranglers. Certainly they were generally older and wiser than most of their contemporaries but they were also smart enough to not allow themselves to get pigeonholed. The angst may have been swept aside by the time the eighties rolled around and 'Golden Brown' exposed them to a wider audience but The Stranglers have never compromised their art and this has allowed them to develop and continue, and above all... endure.

Astonishingly they are now into their fifth decade as a living, breathing band and show no signs of wanting to call it a day. The Men In Black have certainly changed and whilst fans will understandably have a nostalgic devotion to those days of 'Peaches', 'No More Heroes', hot seventies summers and subversiveness, whether it's then or now, The Stranglers continue to delight their loyal following every time they take to the stage.

This book might not excite you as much as JJ's bass lines or Dave's unique keyboard sounds but as a companion piece to the music we hope that it goes some way to adding to your enjoyable Stranglers experiences. At least, long after the memories of those gigs start to fade, this visual delight will remain constant — from the first time you embrace it to the next.

Andy Francis

"It was always the Stranglers against everybody else, but people deserved to be provoked if they were stupid. We did a gig for anti-nuclear power, and Hugh said: 'It's very nice to be here supporting nuclear power.' Of course it all went off. Once we conned someone into booking us for the Young Conservatives. There were 300 people there in penguin suits. Jet went up and said: 'Look, you're not gonna like us so you might as well fuck off now.' Everyone started leaving until there were five people left, who then started following us."
Jean-Jacques Burnel, The Guardian, August 2001

"I liked science. It was a challenge. Music itself is a science, it's got laws, certain progressions. It's a form of mathematics, or at least has a lot in common with mathematics. But I dropped science because I realised I wasn't as good as I needed to be."
Hugh Cornwell, The Word, June 2008

"We were much more violent than any of the other bands because we'd developed a missionary attitude. I wasn't going to let anyone bottle me off stage. In 1976 we did 300 gigs and we were fighting every other night. The other bands were getting the hip press and playing loft parties but we were on the front line. Barricaded in our dressing room in Glasgow. Beaten to a pulp in North Wales. The punks who followed us knew we weren't the "real thing", but the real thing was phonier."
Jean-Jacques Burnel, The Guardian, August 2001

"We weren't aware of being a part of punk; we were just pleased to be gigging. Initially we couldn't get gigs because we weren't considered good enough musicians; after punk we were considered too good. We should have been called the Misfits. Our records were never typically punk, but we had that aggression that came from two years of doing gigs where the audience would throw bottles at us, attack us, or stage mass walk-outs. Nobody who booked us wanted us to play again."
Hugh Cornwell, The Guardian, August 2001

"The demographic started to change. The people who came to see us had shorter hair and were wearing more leather jackets. We were the obvious candidates to support Patti Smith. I remember Joe Strummer was hanging out with us for a bit when he was in a band called The 101ers. They gave us a few gigs at the Elgin when they were moving up to the college circuit and I remember him crying on my shoulder one time when he was really pissed. He said, 'I wish I had a band like yours'!"
Jean-Jacques Burnel, TheQuietus.com, March 2014

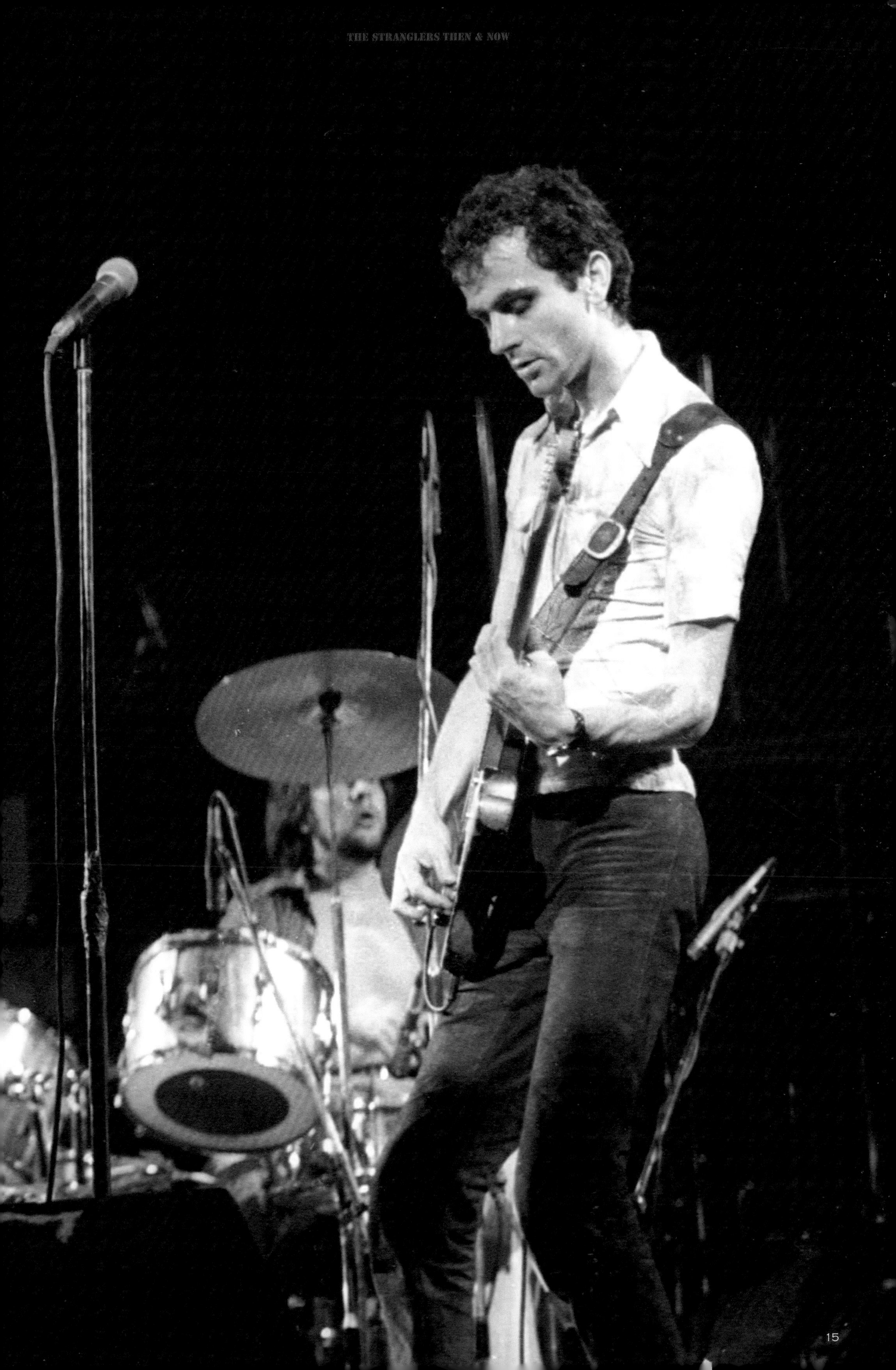

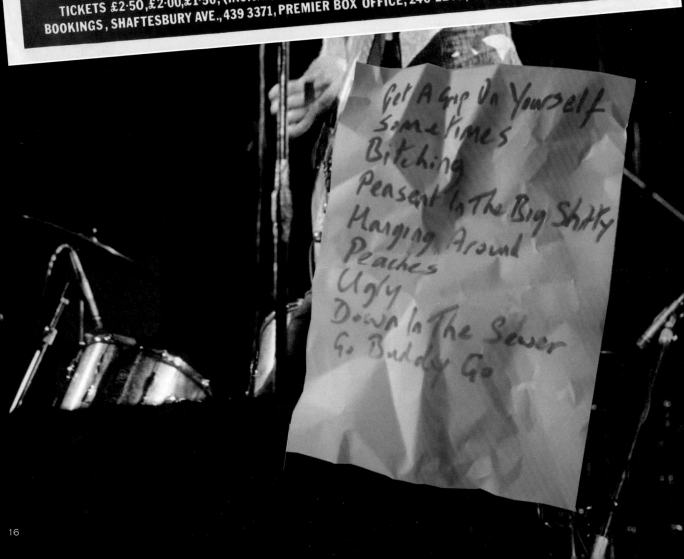

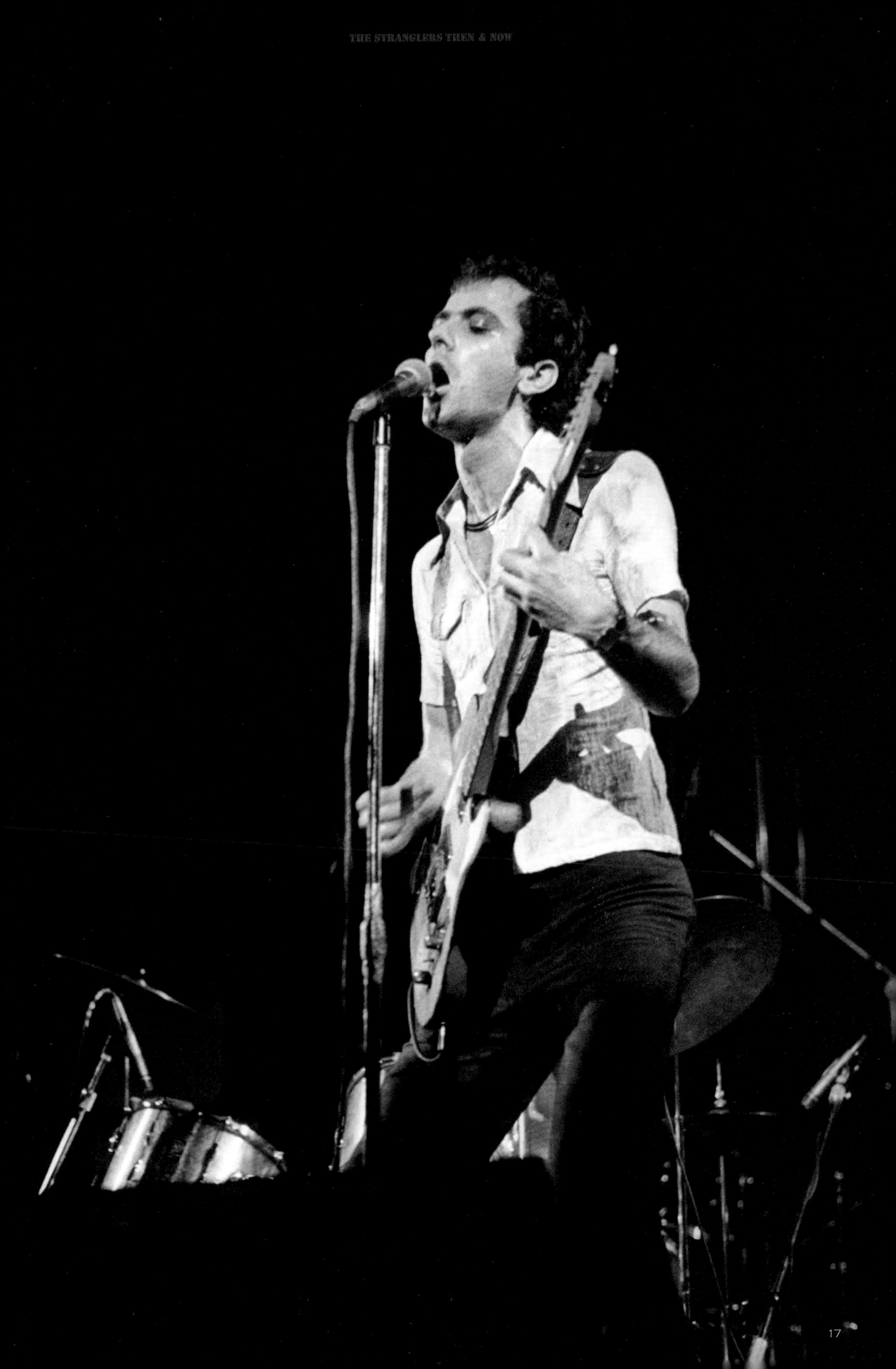

"My aggression was always in the music. I'm not an aggressive person in real life. People are scared of me but I'm very laid back. Jean-Jacques was more aggressive. I preferred to talk the hecklers down but he was more confrontational. We nurtured that aggression because we knew that was the side that helped us."
Hugh Cornwell, The Word, June 2008

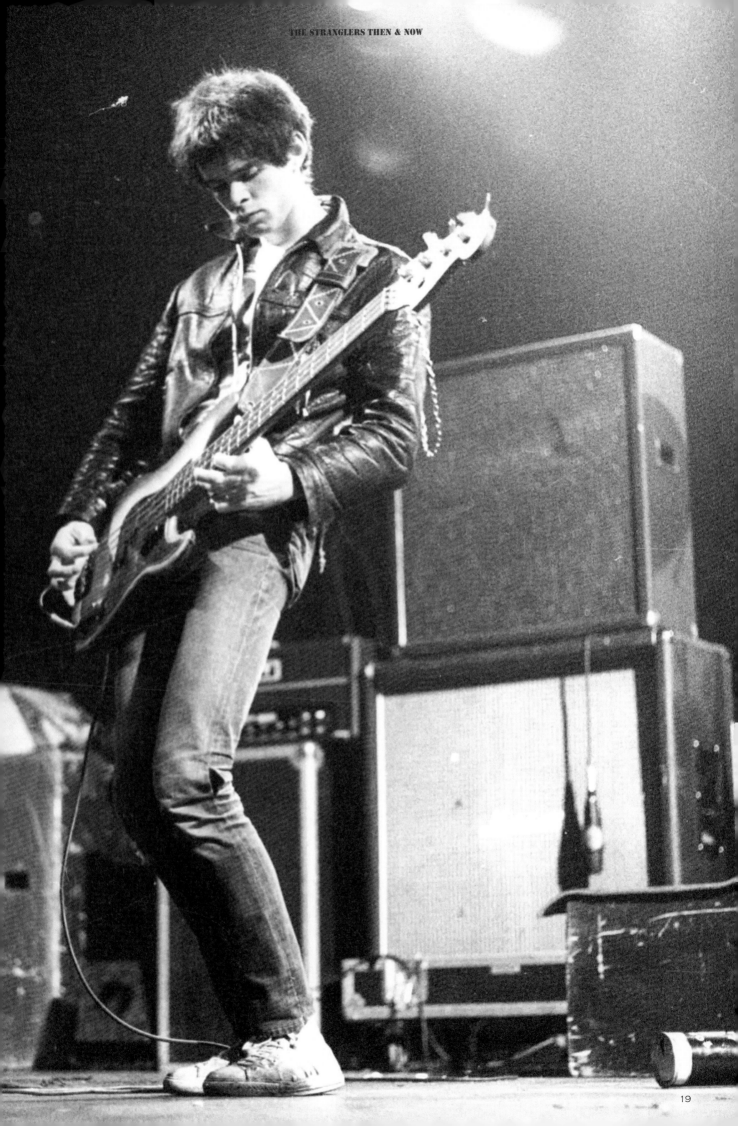

"I was earning about £24 a week which was enough to pay for my bedsit in Guildford and to save a fiver a week towards my ambition. I had a letter of introduction from my karate teacher to go to Japan and that's what I wanted to do. I had this van-driving job and one day, coming back from karate, I gave a lift to some long-haired guy and he turned out to be an American guy who'd come over from Sweden with a band; he was a Vietnam draft dodger and the band had come over to seek their fortune and they ended up living in Guildford above an off-licence owned by a fella called Brian Duffy who then went on to be Jet Black."

Jean-Jacques Burnel, TheQuietus.com, March 2014

Stranglers tour going strong

THE STRANGLERS' tour, which suffered heavily last week at the hands of local councils when several dates were pulled out, survived this week without further mishap and even managed to add one date to their depleted itinery — at Bracknell Sports Centre on June 23.

The group were involved in an incident outside the Canterbury Odeon last week when they went to the aid of two punks who were being beaten up by some other youths, but the police intervened before the fracas got out of hand.

Meanwhile, Albion, the agency who were responsible for breaking many new wave acts, have ceased operations to concentrate on the Stranglers and 999's management and publishing. The Stranglers will shortly be signing an American recording deal with A&M.

FAKE COPS ROB ROXY & STRANGLERS

IN THE EARLY hours of last Sunday morning, the Roxy Club, London's p'nk watering hole, plus Saturday night attraction the Stranglers got ripped off to the tune of the best part of a grand.

After the bus was over and everybody had gone home, Roxy manager Andy and two friends were waiting for the band's three roadies to load equipment into the van out in Neal Street when four characters decked out to resemble refugees from *The Sweeney* appeared on the scene, two of them going straight into the Roxy and the other two approaching the roadies and saying, "Into the club please, we're police officers."

The "cops" flashed their wallets, showing a card with Metropolitan Police cyphered on a crest with white background and both roadies, Andy and friends were taken into the Roxy

and none to politely ushered into Andy's eight-by-four office.

The Stranglers' chief roadie tried to go downstairs to collect his briefcase containing the takings from the previous night's RCA gig, the money from the Roxy gig, PLUS the band's emergency float — in other words, practically everything they got — but the roadie was stopped by the "cops", searched and thrown back in the room before he could get the money . . .

When Andy refused to sit down quietly in a position where he would not be able to see what the "cops" were getting up to in the foyer they forcibly bundled him into a chair. The "cops" took the door keys from Andy and then locked the door from the outside after partaking in a none-too-convincing spate of "cop" talk.

By now it was well apparent that

the "cops" weren't cops at all . . . just professional rip-off merchants . . .

The plaster board wall to the Roxy kitchen was kicked in, somebody scrambled through and released the remaining five locked in the office and within seconds the REAL cops were called — although it was too late to save the briefcase containing the takings of the recent Stranglers gigs, plus their float, a total of £600, PLUS two hundred quid that the Roxy had taken at the door.

When the police arrived they showed Andy and the others what a REAL identification card looked like, as opposed to the ones the hoods were carrying . . . and it seems that it real police I.d. card looks like while we get these thieves in the street . . .

— TONY PARSONS

The Stranglers Glasgow Apollo 16.10.77.

The queue was massive. It crocodiled round three sides of the block and during the long wait the crowd started singing "Pretty Vacant" and "No More Posers". It promised to be some gig. A party of councillors was attending to see if this kind of show was 'suitable', as the concert was almost banned from taking place.

As I entered the hall the support group was already playing. They were those staunch representatives of Scottish new wave The Rezillos. As I took my seat they sang "I Can't Stand My Baby" and the Rolling Stones oldie "I Wanna be your man", both sides of their double B-side single on Sensible Records. Leaving the stage to a hearty applause the bassist said into the mike, "Scotland will rise again." Too right, mate!

During the twenty-minute interval the D.J. got the popgoers warmed up by playing records from the Drones, the Clash and the Dictators.

Eventually the stage darkened and on they walked — the Stranglers — to a deafening roar. They kicked off with their current single "No More Heroes". At the end Hugh Cornwell decided to have a word with the aforementioned councillors. "Where's Mister Aitken and his chums?" he rasped. The crowd shouted with pleasure and a spotlight was put on the council box. Then Hugh said, "Don't judge any other groups by what we do. We don't represent anyone else. We're the Stranglers, right".

From then on the atmosphere grew. They played all their best numbers : "Ugly", "London Lady" ; and a few from their new album such as "Dagenham Dave" and "I Feel like a Wog" with Dave Greenfield taking over lead vocals for "Dead Ringer". The group also did a song I hadn't heard before called "Five Minutes". The show finished all too quickly. It was pure magic. Everyone was out of their seats dancing at the end, we were all shouting for more. After what seemed like years the Stranglers returned to the stage - again to a deafening roar. They played "Peaches" and "Grip" and left the stage for a second time amid whistles and cheers and voices calling for more. Again the group returned and Hugh Cornwell shouted, "Are there any rats here?" There was a positive response and he said, "Good, 'cos this one's for you" and lauched into "Down in the Sewer" with Jean Jacques Burnel pogoing on stage and Hugh creeping round the keyboards with his guitar, looking for rats, no doubt. It was a brilliant number to end on.

"Let's hear your best cheer for the Stranglers," said the DJ and the group finally left the stage to thunderous applause and requests for "Go Buddy Go".

An evening to remember.

Kenneth Lindsay

Anachronism In The U.K.

Jean-Jacques Burnel

Pic: GUS STEWART

The Stranglers
The Only Ones
CAMBRIDGE

WHATEVER HAPPENED to — the existentialist heroes, or the de Niroes?

It's true: for most people there are no more heroes — only group therapy. Safety in numbers — dress by numbers, dance by numbers.

Straight in to all of this come the Only Ones, who live up to the name, sort of. Lead singer Peter Perret wears mascara and sings in a way redolent of an affectionate parody of Steve Harley. Lead guitarist John Perry plays solo, man, plays them slow, with sustain rather than disdain. Drummer Mike Kellie is apparently something of a veteran, like Jet Black of The Stranglers, the inconspicuous and reliable type. Bassist Alan Mair is the only bow in the direction of Blank, with his tight leather liquorice stick trousers.

Collectively, they seem to really phase the crowd — switching from Ramoneish tempo of attack, to a slower, more thoughtful approach, Perry's guitar terse and understated, an odd snatch of lyric making you think in terms of *potential*. But as people nearer the band than I remarked, they have to decide exactly where they are aiming.

My all too Western mind was plagued with preconception over The Stranglers — yes, that's right, the sexist bit. Well, almost, because my objections were never motivated by any Crusading Spirit for the, er, sisters — just that I've always found any manifestations on the Macho-see Macho-do projection in Pop Kulture to be somewhat infantile.

Having said that — blow for sainthood — they came over about as sexist as the National

Front are humanist. In fact they came over as nothing if not bored, little or no effort made to win over the crowd with sexist remarks or otherwise and atmosphere less-than-zero. As the set wore on I began to realize that the Only Ones weren't the only ones, anachronism-wise. I mean these guys are strange heroes — no short back and spikes, no contempo "This City Will Be The Death Of Me" imagery, and Greenfield playing with increasing weirdness on the ivorys — psychedelia rampant for a change of gear (velocity) and a dance that doesn't hammer the Law of Gravity with such force.

As for the music, I found it all a bit sick and detached. They may be more accomplished instrumentally than the majority of the New Wave, but they don't seem to play with any conviction, live force. Certainly not enough light and shade. They played "Straighten Out", "Bring On The Nubiles", "Sometimes", "Dagenham Dave", "Dead Ringer" (everyone greeting it, apparently as "Peaches" which they didn't play), "Hanging Around", "Peasant In The Big Shitty", "I Feel Like A Wog", a new song "Five Minutes", "London Lady", "No More Heroes" and "Something Better Change".

Somewhere into "Grip", the first number of the "encore", two "Chicks" materialised on stage and proceeded to do what can best be described as a mindless, formless, moron-cheer leader dance, going on to clutch Cornwall and Burnel in a manner that would have made Woody and Les envious. No attempt was made to get rid of them, even by the heavies or The Stranglers themselves — who looked as if they were past caring. More and more people followed suit on to the stage until the band — by now plowing through an unscheduled (?) instrumental (?) — was totally obscured by the frenzied mob.

Ian Penman

Stranglers Roundhouse

IT'S DIFFICULT to know where to start. I mean, I could tell you about the queue of people almost 100 yards long that had to be turned away because the Roundhouse was full up. And I could waste a line or two on the Jam. Paul Weller and Bruce Foxton in their black suits, right legs pumping Beatles-style, Rickenbacker guitars slung round their necks, and Rick Buckler at the drums turning on high-energy Who that justly earned the Jam the kind of encore the Roundhouse rarely affords the band at the bottom.

Or else I could try a thumbnail sketch of Cherry Vanilla (getting a little fat my dear) but with her wild red hair, black stockings, and gold lame hotpants, walking on the wild side of high camp cabaret.

But it was the Stranglers who topped the bill. I've never seen them play good gigs and I've seen diabolical ones, but I've never seen them approach the heights they scaled at the Roundhouse on their first headlining appearance in a major London venue.

They rise to the occasion with the best set I've ever seen them play. How many promising young bands have you seen burn themselves out once they gain mass acceptance. Too many, right? Not so the Stranglers. Of course, they aired many of the tracks from their debut album, 'IV (Rattus Norvegicus)' how could they gig without 'Peaches', 'Grip', 'Down In The Sewer' or 'Sometimes'. But it was new ones like 'Straighten Out', 'Whatever Happened To The Hero' and the amazing 'I Feel Like A Wog' (realism not racism) that will decide their future.

Confident to the point of arrogance, the Stranglers dominated a packed house of screaming, gesticulating and pogo-ing kids. Loud and clear, they mixed vital, intense New Wave beat with moments of pure psychedelia that would put Pink Floyd or Hawkwind to shame. Hugh Cornwell and Jean-Jacques Burnel hosied down the audience like urban guerillas, while behind them Dave Greenfield washed the stage with a steady torrent of bubbling and boiling organs chords that added colour to Jet Black's heart attack drumming.

If the Stranglers play many more gigs like this, they will be huge before the summer's out, mark my words. — Chas de Whalley.

STRANGLERS: they will be huge

Never take sweets from a Strangler

CHAS DE WHALLEY

"We've always had to respond to circumstances. We have had a lot of people who have believed what they've read about us in the tabloid press and come spoiling for a fight — and you've got to defend yourself."
Jet Black, Oxford Times, March 2014

KYRKJARARNIR ENDUÐU Í LÆKNUM

Frá hljómleikunum. Eftir samkvæmi í Hollywood fóru kapparnir í bað í læknum í Nauthólsvík, og þótti sumum tími til kominn.

Um fjögur þúsund og fimm hundruð ungmenni komu í Laugardalshöllina á miðvikudagskvöldið, til þess að sjá og heyra bresku „Kyrkjarana", The Stranglers og íslensku hljómsveitirnar Póker og Þursaflokkinn og Halla og Ladda.

Reyndar tókst ekki sem skyldi með þessa tónleika — að sögn vegna slæmrar framkomu Stranglers-manna. Þursaflokkurinn, sem léku átti á tónleikunum, gerði það ekki, vegna þess ábekki var tími til að prófa hljómtæki. Hljómsveitarinnar Stranglers tóku nefnilega miklu lengri tíma til sinnar prófunar, en þeim hafði verið úthlutað.

Egill Ólafsson kom fram í

byrjun tónleikanna og sagði frá því hvernig málum væri komið, en síðan tóku Halli og Laddi við.

Hljómsveitin Póker lék svo af tveim fyrri hljómsveitum sín-um — hvaðbannst grafhesta-rokk, sem féll íslenska punk-unkunni vel í geð. Nokkrir ung-ingana máttu með „..kikkar-hots"naður í gegnum nef neða kinu, og máladur tilheyrandi lit-um.

Eftir tónleikana sagði gítar-leikarinn Hugh Cornwell hljóm-sveitarfélögum sanggða með hljómleikana. „Fólkið virtist skemmta sér vel, við skemmt-um okkur vel og er þá yfir nokkru að kvarta?" sagði hann í samtali við Vísi eftir tónleikana.

Fyrr um daginn hafði ný plata Stranglers — „Black and White" verið kynnt fyrir heims-

En það voru Stranglers sem beðið var eftir. Nokkur úgvum var í salnum, og stemningin góð, hvort sem það var áfengið að kenna eða ekki.

Að tónleikunum læknum átti að fara í bað í Hollywood, en af ein-hverjum ástæðum voru Kyrkjararnir látnir bíða til í rúma í klukku-tíma áður en hleypt var inn. Kápparnir héldust svo þétt að áðeins tveir jeðru bíru sig, hinir fóru heim. A myndinni er tromsnarinn í rúmmi, og ekki alltof hress. Vísinmyndir BP.

Íslensk ungmenni „Hollu" Stranglers í botn.

presuunni í samkvæmi í Skifla-skalanum í liverudölum. Platan er svipuð tveim þeim fyrri, en virkaði þó lítu betur leikin og vandaðri.

Erlendu blaðamennirnir tóku henni vel og sumir spáðu að Stranglers myndu sla í gegn með honni. Ljóst er að tónleik unum í gærkvöldi að þeir hafa þegar slegið í gegn á Íslandi, svo þá er hara restin af heimin-um eftir.

Í gær var á æður að fara á hesthak en eins og fyrri daginn reyndu Stranglers ekki að taka þátt í leiknum. Gítarleikarinn fór reyndar til Kaupmanna-hafnar í gærmorgun og tromm-arinn fór á bak, en hinir tveir sváfu fram eftir degi.

Öll hersngin, að undanskild-um tveim eða þeim rökurum héllt síðan aleiðis til Oslo síðdeg-is í gær. —GA

Tíminn   Sunnudagur 7. maí 1978.

22

Nútíminn ★ ★ ★

Dave Greenfield fór á kostum í hljómborðsleik. Tímamyndir Róbert.   Það var þröngt á þingi er Stranglers léku lagið „Down in the Sewer".

Stranglers slógu í gegn

Stranglers lifa meðan þeir hafa eitthvað að segja

FRÆGASTI TOLLARINN TÓK Á MÓTI KYRKJURUNUM

STRANGLERS, brezka hljómsveitin sem kemur fram í tónleikum í kvöld í Reykjavík, kom til landsins í gær. Á myndinni tekur Kristján Pétursson frægasti tollvörður landsins á móti þeim. „Kyrkjararnir" eins og nafn þeirra mun útleggjast fóru um græna hliðið og í farangri þeirra þurfti ekkert að róta. Á myndinni er Kristján Pétursson fyrir innan borðið, en brezku hljómlistar-mennirnir fyrir utan. — DB-mynd Ragnar Th. Sig. Sjá bls. 15.

THE STRANGLERS THEN & NOW

STRANGLERS GET A LONDON GO-AHEAD FOR OPEN-AIR SHOW

THE STRANGLERS have finally fixed their London show. The group will play an open-air show at Battersea Park on September 16, heading a four-band bill that includes at least one major non-new wave band.

Tickets at £4.00 a head are being limited to 8,000 and will be available from September 1, the day after the licences for the concert are due to be finally passed.

A special stage has been designed for the show — it will be put in the middle of the site, allowing all-round vision so that no one in the audience will be more than 120 feet from the bands. Promoter Harvey Goldsmith will he using the same stage canopy as at Blackbushe, and the p.a. will be stored under the stage.

Tickets will be available from Harlequin Records in London, Harvey Goldsmith's box office at Chappells in New Bond Street, and usual agents. Car parking will be available near the site at the Chelsea Bridge entrance, but no camping will be allowed.

30

"By the time we played Battersea Park, 'No More Heroes' had been Top 10 and we'd been accused of being sexist. My girlfriend at the time lived in Acton with her sister and a girl called Linda who was a stripper. They came to my defence. Linda was a professional stripper and she said, 'Can I strip to your song 'Nice And Sleazy'?' so we said, 'Yeah' and she did it in Brighton. As the furore around the sexism accusation increased, she said, 'I've got quite a few girls who'd love to strip at this Battersea show you're going to do.' And my girlfriend's sister, who was 16 at the time, she wasn't a stripper but she said, 'I want to show who is empowered here' so she volunteered. So we had a line-up of four professional strip girls and Jane, my girlfriend's sister. So it was their decision to do it and then of course we got accused of exploiting them!"

Jean-Jacques Burnel,
TheQuietus.com, March 2014

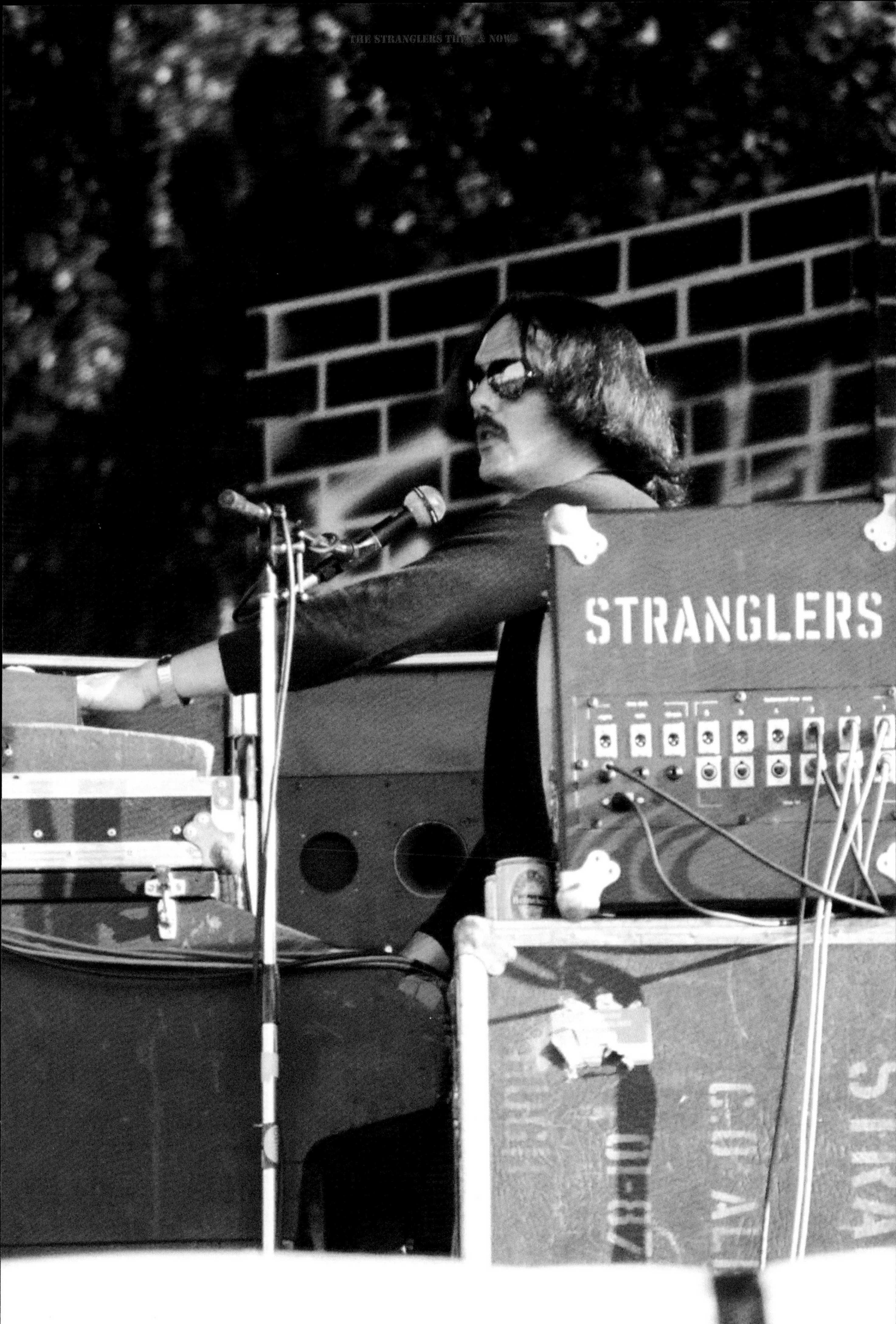
STRANGLERS

*"My crew were a group of guys called The Finchley Boys.
They also worked with the Stranglers and Toyah Wilcox."*
**Hazel O'Connor
(from her autobiography *Breaking Glass Barefoot*)**

"In the early days people hated us — but there was a certain excitement about that. We've always felt it's cool to be different."
Jet Black, Oxford Times, March 2014

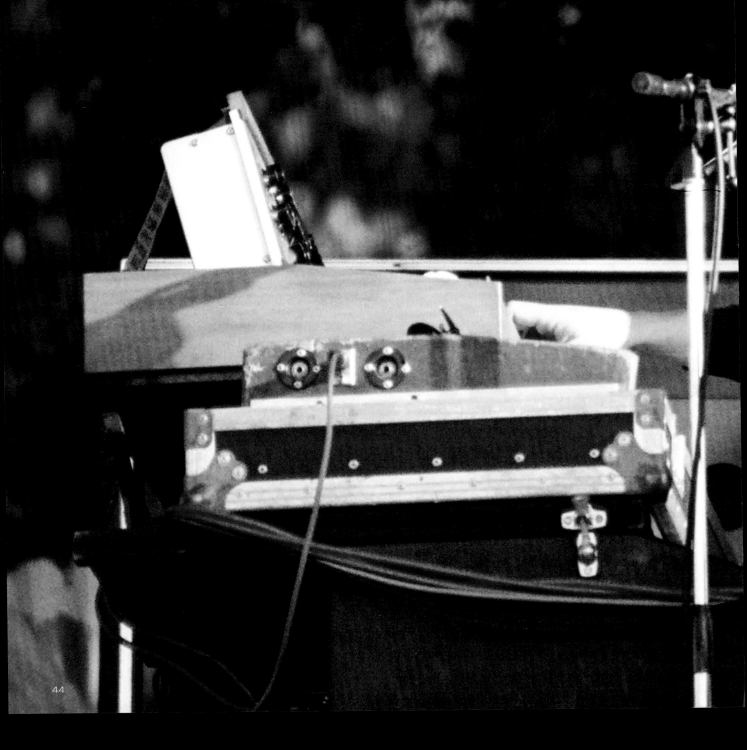

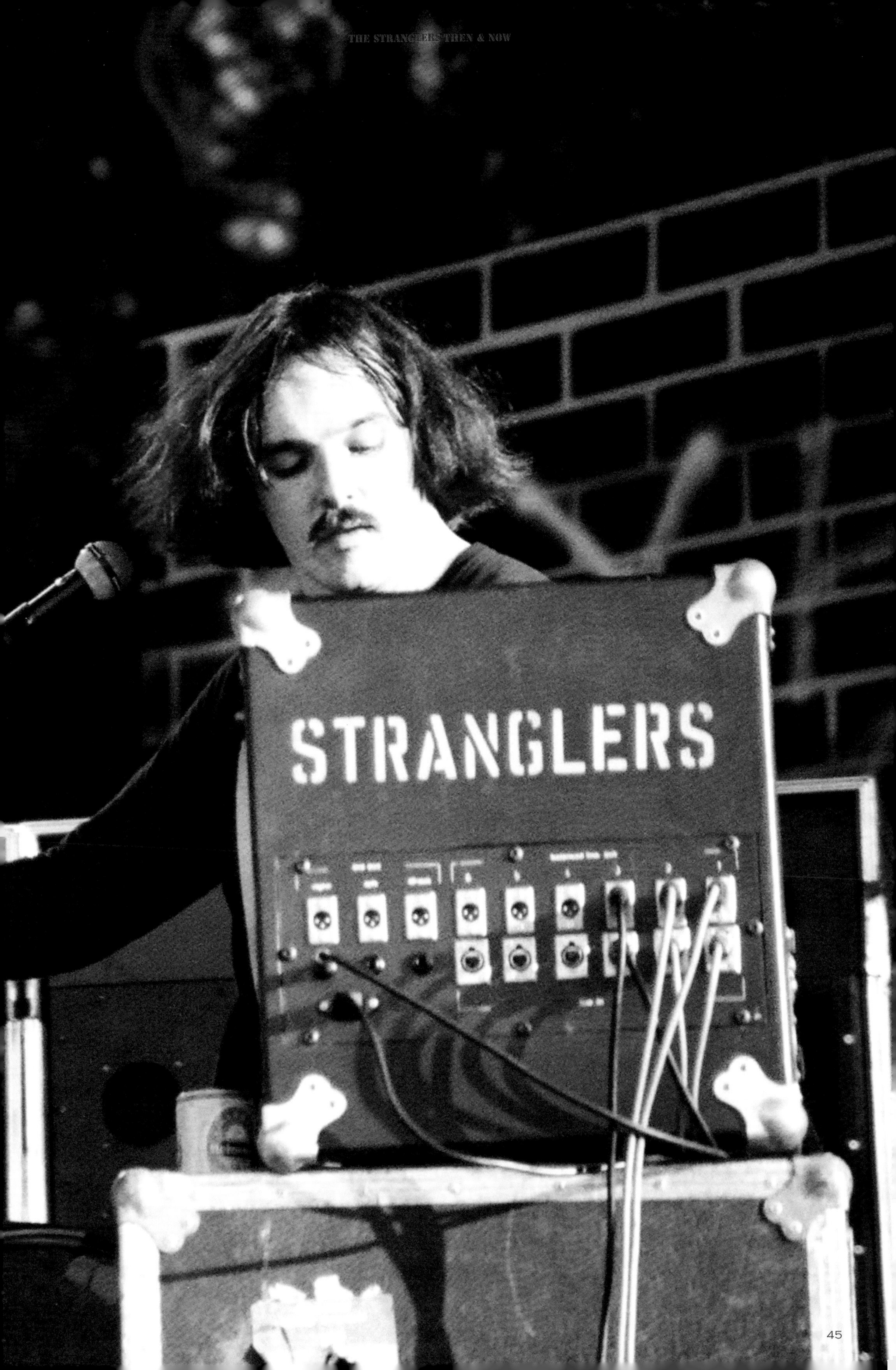
STRANGLERS

*"The last song on the set was 'Nice'n'Sleazy'. We hired twenty
strippers to come on stage with us, all professionals.
Afterwards the police tried to arrest them all but they weren't
quite sure how to do it. They didn't handcuff any of them,
they just took their numbers and that was the last of it."*
Hugh Cornwell, The Guardian, August 2001

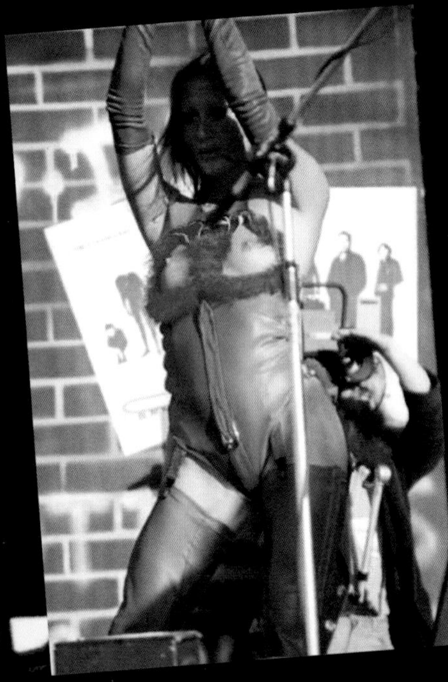

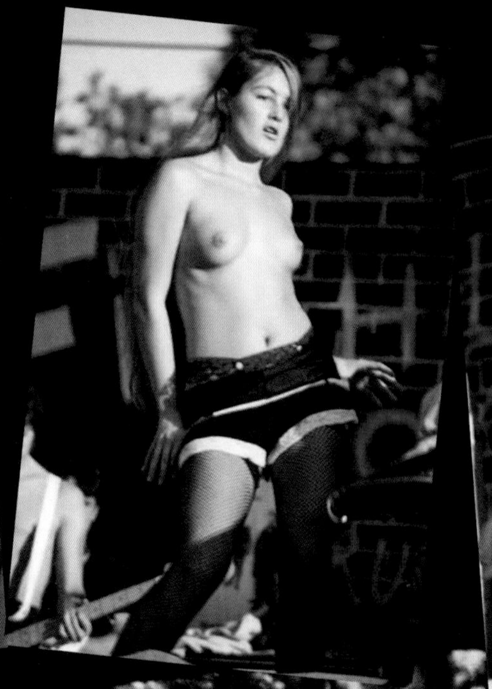

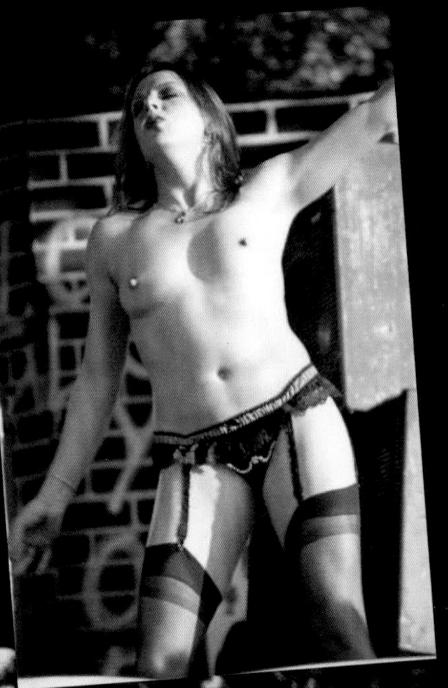

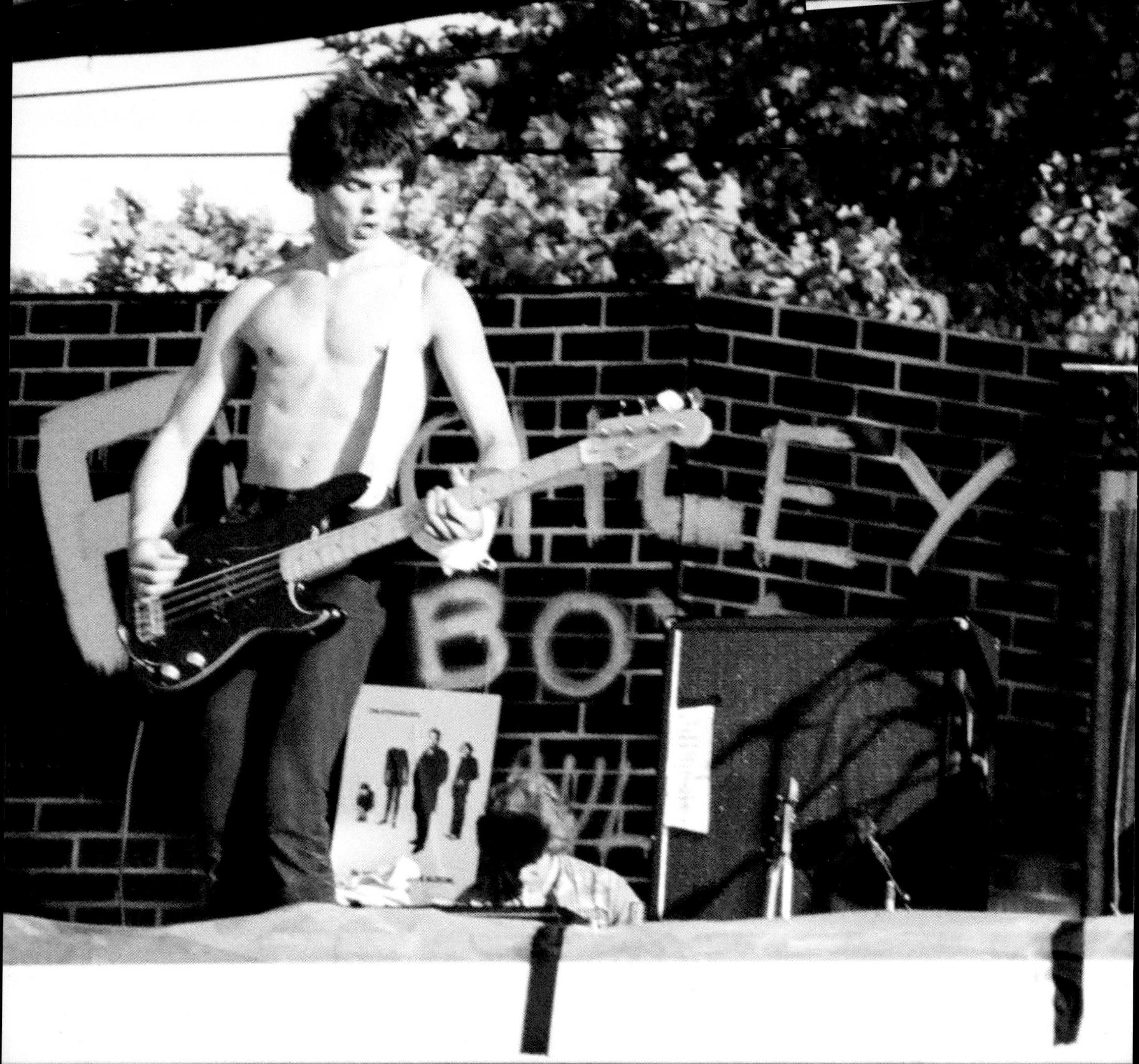

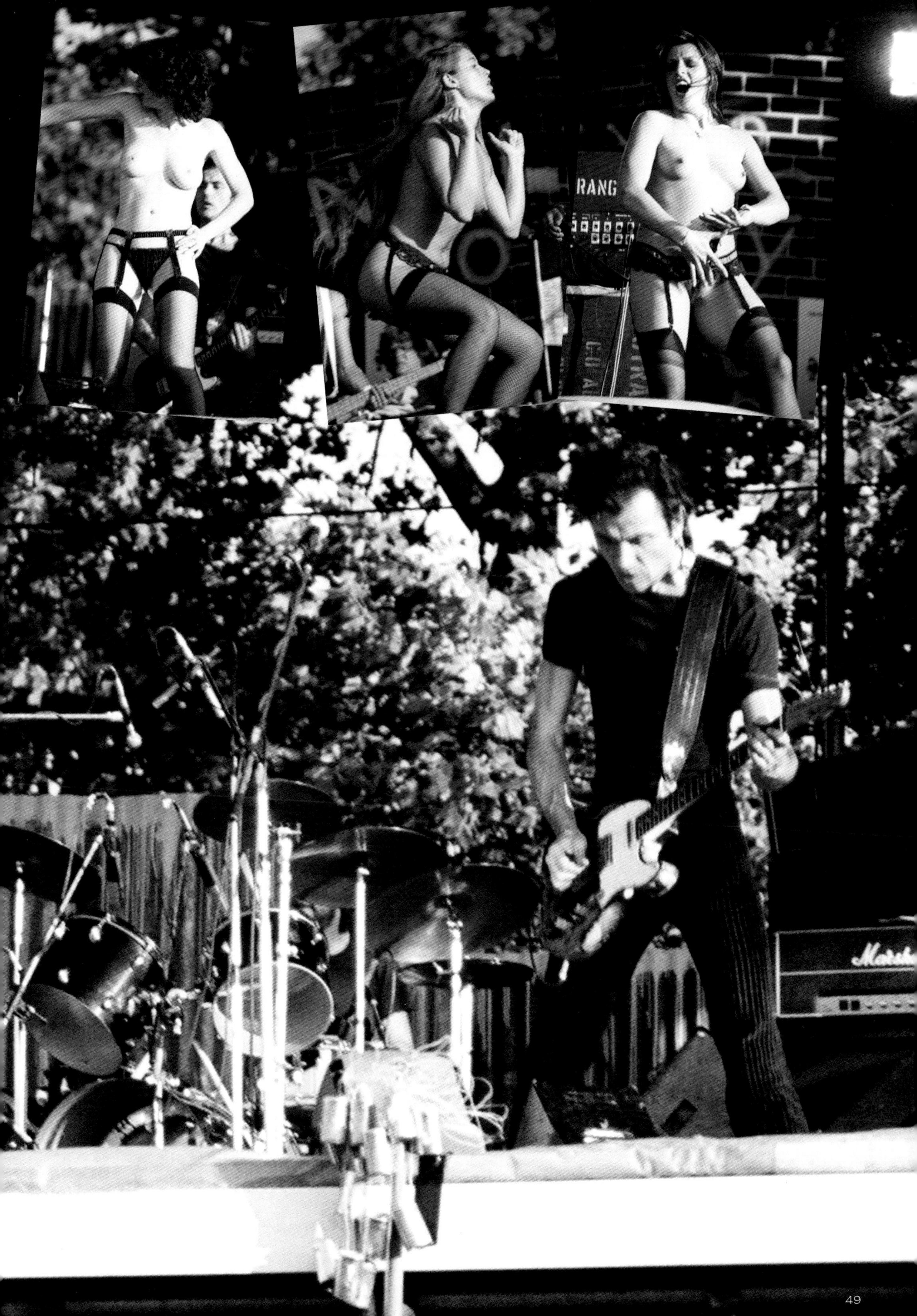

"We avoided selling our souls to the American market. We started doing quite well there playing to 5,000 people a night and I couldn't stand it. The longest we did in America was three months and we used to go once or twice a year and it was doing my head in. I just didn't like it very much. I missed my girlfriend and one time I came back from three months in America and it took six months to lose all the weight I put on!"
Jean-Jacques Burnel,
TheQuietus.com, March 2014

"For a little while I went out with Hugh but he had been busted for drugs and a week after we began our romance he was sent to prison for two months — the judge was making an example of him. Whilst Hugh was in prison, the Stranglers had a big London gig to do at the Rainbow Theatre and no lead singer, so they invited other singers and musicians to do a few songs each. I did 'Grip' and 'Hanging Around', with a very young Robert Smith of The Cure playing guitar."
Hazel O'Connor (from her autobiography _Breaking Glass Barefoot_)

"*In France they treat us as intellectuals whereas here they treat us as mischievous yobs I suppose.*"
Hugh Cornwell, *Rapido*, French TV, February 1990

"You always need every sort of instrument even though now you can get exactly the same sounds on a keyboard but the actual technique of playing... especially brass instruments. I could probably get exactly the same sound of certain things, say a trombone. But the breathing would always be the same as stored and for me to play it would be like playing a trumpet with a keyboards outlook... a keyboard style. In other words a true trombone or trumpet player would work out his own riffs and play something totally different to what I would think of to play."
Dave Greenfield,
Stranglers In The Night,
French TV special 1985

"One recent journalist described us as misfits and I think he was probably right. We are misfits; we don't fit into the system of things so I suppose we are noticeable."
Jet Black, *Rapido*, French TV, February 1990

"We started when most bands are retiring."
Jean-Jacques Burnel, *Rapido*, French TV, February 1990

Stranglers' Ally Pally plan sinks

STRANGLERS' main London appearance during their current world tour has been cancelled after continuous licensing problems with the GLC. The band has had to abandon plans for shows at London's Alexandra Palace or QPR football ground, and is now offering free transport to anyone from the London area who buys tickets for the group's show at Stafford's Bingley Hall on May 30. Tickets are available from Chappell's in New Bond Street, London. Album: p26.

THE STRANGLERS, whose world tour plans were announced by MM last week, have run into a major problem in their attempt to organise a main London show for the British section of the tour.

The band has been trying to arrange a big London venue for their show, and last week it was hoped to play two nights at London's Alexandra Palace to a total of around 12,000 people, but now it looks as if the Alexandra Palace plans are definitely off following difficulties with the GLC. Promoter Paul Loasby, for Harvey Goldsmith, is having problems finding an alternative hall for the shows.

Loasby is saying little about the difficulties except to admit that there is a big problem about Alexandra Palace and other venues. He hopes that something will be sorted out within a fortnight.

A GLC spokesman said the Alexandra Palace proposal had been turned down because to have 6,000 people in a hall without seats would pose a threat to public safety they could not accept.

The first three British Stranglers dates are at Brighton, Glasgow and Stafford in late May, and follow the start of the band's world tour in Iceland on May 3. The tour closes on July 16 at Las Palmas in the Canary Islands.

The British shows so far confirmed are: Brighton Centre (May 20), Glasgow Apollo (26) and Stafford New Bingley Hall (30), and tickets are now available for the shows.

● Promoter Harvey Goldsmith faced more GLC last week. The original arr... farewell show at the London Rai... removal of the first ten rows.

Shortly before the show the... rows could be removed. As a re... badly damaged during the con...

Nice 'n' Sleazy

THE STRANGLERS NEW SINGLE ● NICE 'N' SLEAZY/SHUT

Stranglers night in Brighton cells

THE STRANGLERS were involved in another incident with the police last week, resulting in two of them — drummer Jet Black and bassist Jean Jaques Burnel — being detained overnight in the cells, and subsequently being charged with disorderly conduct.

The trouble started after the band's gig last Wednesday night at Brighton Top Rank, when six policemen and a dog stormed into their dressing room, only to leave after they had looked the place over. Apparently a large number of police had attended the concert, because about two dozen Hells Angels from Holland — whom the Stranglers had befriended when touring that country — were in the audience.

The band and their entourage returned to their hotel (followed by two police cars), where they learned that two of their Dutch friends had been detained by the

It's claimed that offers of bail were not taken seriously and, as the result of alleged obstruction on the premises, the three were arrested and spent the night in the cells. They were released the following morning after they had each paid £25 bail, and manager Ian Grant contributed £50 per person. They are due to appear in court at Brighton on November 15 to face the charges.

Jet Black, claiming he was not allowed to use the phone or medicine he needed, commented:

"We're all perpl... activity in Brigh... Grant went furth... the police of "deli... tion".

The Stranglers... getting used to t... tions. Recently... hotel, in which th... was raided twice... police.

ROCKAB
FOR BR

ROADSHOWS

old c

THE STRANGLERS playing at the Red Cow

CORNWELL QUITS THE STRANGLERS

● "Bugger this," says Hugh. "I'm off!" — but rest of the band carry on regardless

TWO SIDES of vintage Hugh: dark and reflective, and (inset) live '77 (Live pic: Gus Stewart)

STRANGLERS' VOCALIST, guitarist and founder member Hugh Cornwell has quit the band after almost 17 years — making the Stranglers' recent appearance at London's Alexandra Palace the last with the original band line-up.

But despite his departure, The Stranglers will continue as a band and will be seeking a replacement.

Cornwell intends to pursue a career in acting — he was recently seen in the cinema commercial for a brand of tequila, directed by video brat Tim Pope — and will also be working on solo music projects.

"I've enjoyed all my years with The Stranglers," Hugh said last week. "But all good things have to come to an end someday. We've just released what I think is one of the band's strongest LPs — 'Ten' — and the gig at Ally Pally was so good, I thought,

Well, if I'm ever going to go, I should go now while I'm ahead.

"Although I think I may have surprised the rest of the band with this announcement, there is no bad feeling between us and the parting is completely amicable."

Fellow founding Strangler Jean Jacques Burnel said: "Of course, we tried everything to make him stay — Chinese water torture, placing lighted matches under his fingernails, all the usual Stranglers methods of persuasion, but it was no good; he'd made his decision and was determined to stick by it! The Stranglers are always changing. This is just another change we're going through."

But Burnel's dismissive comment seems somewhat bizarre: the band's line-up hasn't changed since they rose to fame in 1977!

Stranglers manager Colin Johnson said: "Obviously we're sad that Hugh is leaving, but there are no plans to disband the group. We shall be scouring the country for a suitable replacement, but in the meantime we wish Hugh all the best."

They hope to have a replacement by the autumn and be on the road in early 1991.

The Stranglers are one of the most durable bands of the punk era — in fact until Cornwell's departure they were the only ones who'd stayed together this long! Formed in 1974, they used to tour in drummer Jet Black's ice cream van. They signed to United Artists in 1976, releasing their first single, 'London Lady'/'Grip', in time to be regarded as part of the burgeoning punk scene. Their first LP 'Rattus Norvegicus IV' was essential listening when released in 1977.

Stranglers, Jam hit by violence in Scandinavia

THE STRANGLERS' massive 36-date tour opens on schedule at Cambridge tomorrow (Friday), though the first few gigs looked to be in jeopardy until a few days ago, after the band were viciously attacked in Sweden and two members of their road crew were taken to hospital.

The incident occurred when the Stranglers were set upon by gangs of thugs belonging to a semi-political group called the Regeris, who are described as a cross between the National Front and Hell's Angels. All the band were battered, and £3,000 worth of their equipment was a write-off — including their amps and Jean Jacques Burnel's guitar, which was broken in half.

The fracas was front-page news in all the Swedish daily papers, coming soon after a similar — though not so severe — attack on the Sex Pistols during their recent tour of that country. Not surprisingly, the Stranglers cancelled the rest of their dates in Sweden, and flew home last

Thursday. Although still shaken, they are going ahead with their British tour as planned.

The band's first album "TV Rattus Norvegicus" officially went Gold this week. It is still strongly placed in the Top Thirty after 22 weeks and, based upon the NME Annual Chart Points Table, it is currently the eighth best-selling album of the year — with every likelihood of this placing being improved.

THE JAM also encountered violence in Sweden when, in Ronneby last weekend, the audience started pelting them with eggs and chair legs after their first number. This was followed by a stage invasion, when their bank of speakers was knocked over and seriously damaged.

The band beat a hasty retreat and didn't complete their set. Because of the damage to their gear, they were forced to cancel Sunday's gig in Stockholm and a concert in Holland on Wednesday.

The Jam fly to America next week for a short introductory promotional tour, during which

they will be playing at such prestige venues as Los Angeles Whiskey, New York CBGB's and Boston The Rat. Paul Weller is also guesting with Iggy Pop in NBC-TV's 'Tomorrow' show, which will include film of the band playing live at Manchester Electric Circus.

To tie in with their visit, 40 F.M. radio stations will be playing hour-long live recordings of The Jam performing at London Nashville and 100 Club. The band then fly direct to the Continent to complete their European schedule, and it is understood that selected British dates are planned for November.

STRANGLERS-ROCK'S SEXIST PIGS

They're Rock's Bad Boys—and for once it isn't a pose. The Stranglers are just maybe as mean as they seem

Stranglers deny 'split'

THE STRANGLERS this week denied reports in the London *Evening News* that they're considering splitting up. The story quoted Jean Jacques Burnel as saying they were all sick and tired of the criticisms being levelled against them, and that too many people were after their blood. "We don't want to split, but the situation looks bad" was one of his alleged quotes.

But this week Burnel explained that he'd been "taking the *Evening News* for a ride". He told NME: "There's no way we shall be breaking up, and no way anyone can break us up."

Burnel is also directly involved in what may be a "Top Of The Pops" ban on The Stranglers. It seems he broke down a dressing

New Wave Produ
A&M Recording Sta

...ntensity of rea
punk
rock

Sunday, A
Stone

The STRANGLERS & friends
vs.
The Media

THE CRICKET MATCH OF THE CENTURY !!
...Sunday 16 Sept-Paddington Recreation Ground-
Randolph Ave., London W9 (Tube: Maida Vale)
Free admission....collection for Help a London Child
Frolics, fun, food, fresh air, famous faces....Be there!

...ttus Norvegicus, th
...nd turned heads in
...More Heroes, is rea
...of razor's-edge roc
...s is not just makin
...e Stranglers will

...RS Album
...$4.88.

...NGLERS
...ison, Sun. April

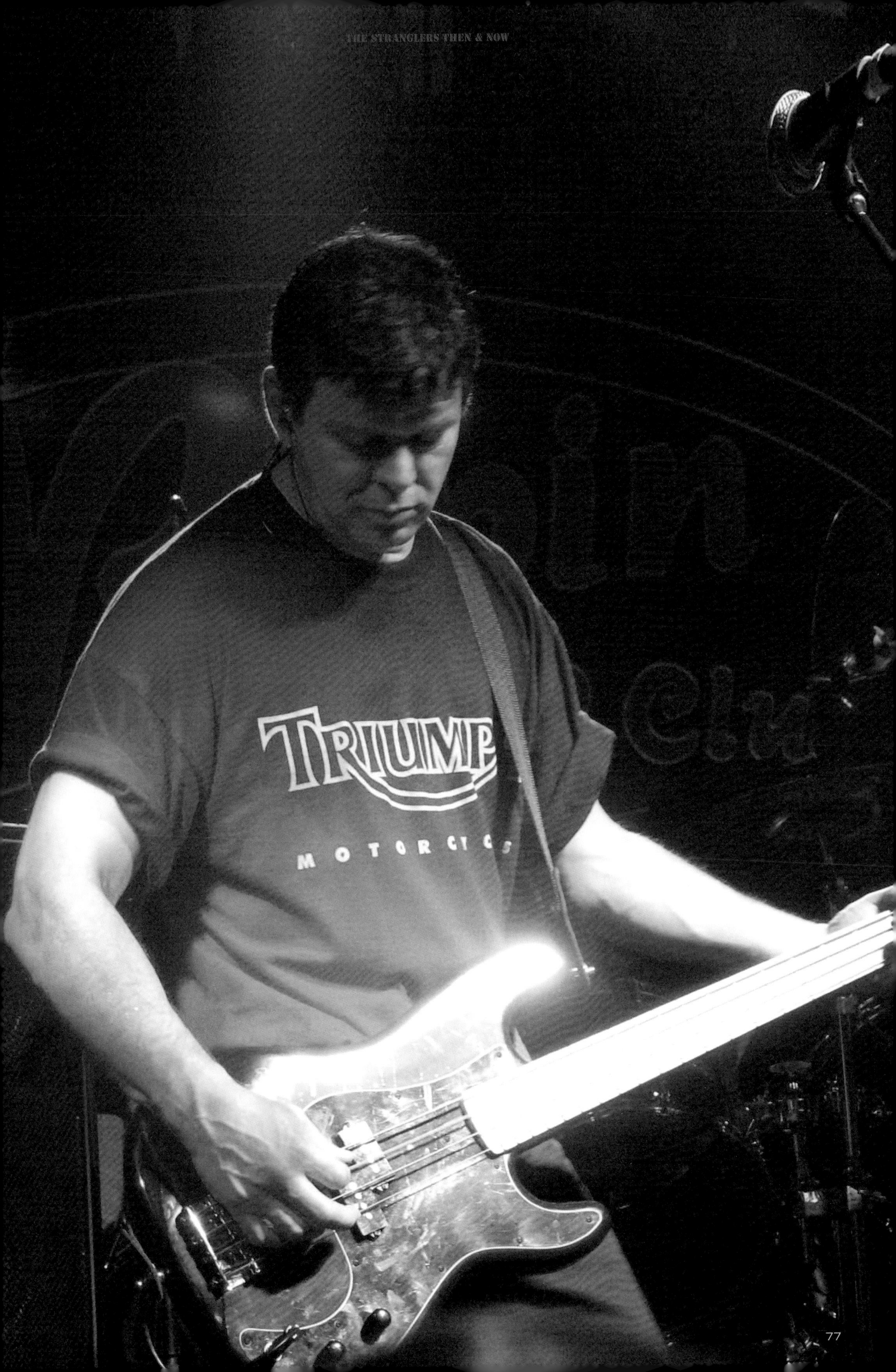
TRIUMP

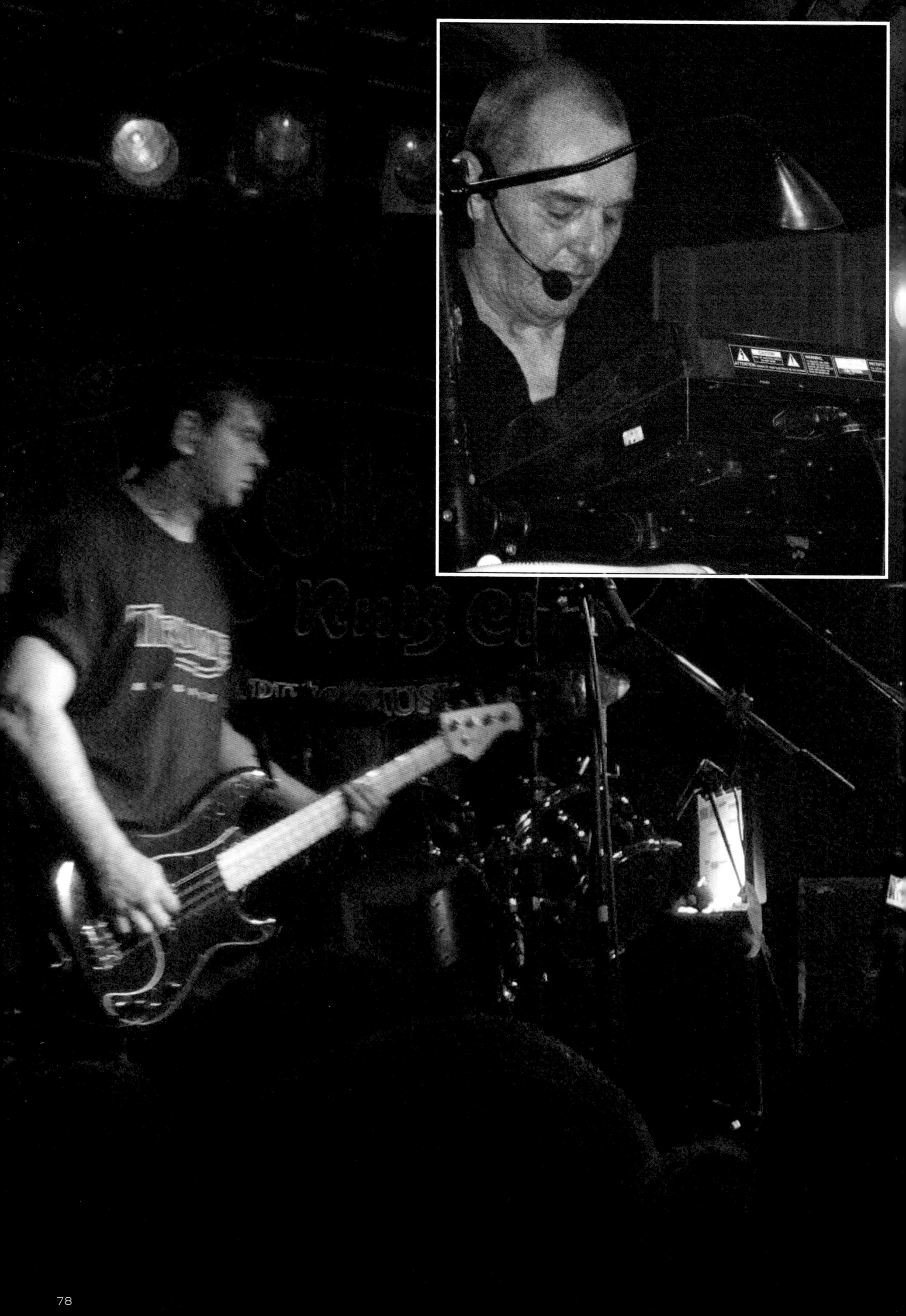

"I'm really happy now the way things are going. When we released the first album I was on, Norfolk Coast, *that was a long process. I joined in 2000 but the album didn't come out until 2004. So it took us a while to find the direction for that. I would have liked it to go in a more heavier kind of rocky direction. Ultimately, through a long process of writing, we wrote all the songs from scratch, and we went out on the road and played them all live as well, which was a huge factor on that record."*
Baz Warne, Yorkshire Magazine, 2017

THE STRANGLERS THEN & NOW

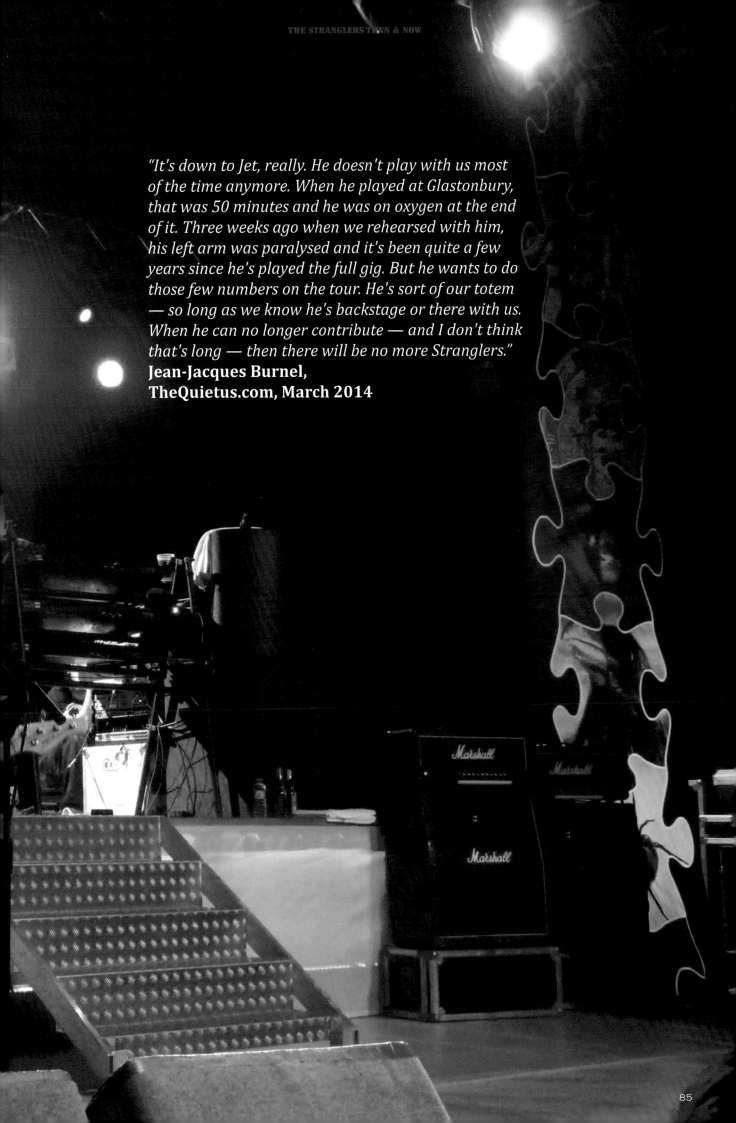

"It's down to Jet, really. He doesn't play with us most of the time anymore. When he played at Glastonbury, that was 50 minutes and he was on oxygen at the end of it. Three weeks ago when we rehearsed with him, his left arm was paralysed and it's been quite a few years since he's played the full gig. But he wants to do those few numbers on the tour. He's sort of our totem — so long as we know he's backstage or there with us. When he can no longer contribute — and I don't think that's long — then there will be no more Stranglers."
**Jean-Jacques Burnel,
TheQuietus.com, March 2014**

"I did feel that I belonged immediately. Obviously they have a huge history. They were very tight. It's like coming into a huge, big bloody entity. I mean I didn't know the band or the crew. The only thing I did know was the songs. But I was welcomed in with open arms. We've been very fast, tight friends from the word go.

I think when I proved my worth, if you like, was with some of the songs that I'd written and attitude and just the way that I approach things. It seemed to fit in very well with them. Plus I'm quite significantly younger and I'm from an entirely different part of the country. They're southerners and I'm a northern boy. I know it sounds a bit silly, but there was something to be said for that as well. Bringing everybody back down to earth a little bit."
Baz Warne, Yorkshire Magazine, 2017

TTD
GO B GO
GRIP
CURFEW
NORFOLK
SKIN
SUN
SLUG
GB
CONTROL
RETRO
GENETIX
SLEAZY
PEACHES
SPECTRE
WALK
NUKE
DUCHESS
SEWER

5 MINS · WWW – CHANGE
HA · HE

THE STRANGLERS THEN & NOW

"There are big rock star moments then there is going into Asda to do your shopping. We're just people at the end of the day. We do enjoy the trappings from time to time. I'd be a liar if I said we didn't."
Baz Warne, Yorkshire Magazine, 2017

"

*"No, we don't keep in touch. That's not on purpose, though. I just
don't think about it too much. We have a brilliant frontman with
Baz and Hugh decided to do something different."*
Jet Black, Oxford Times, March 2014

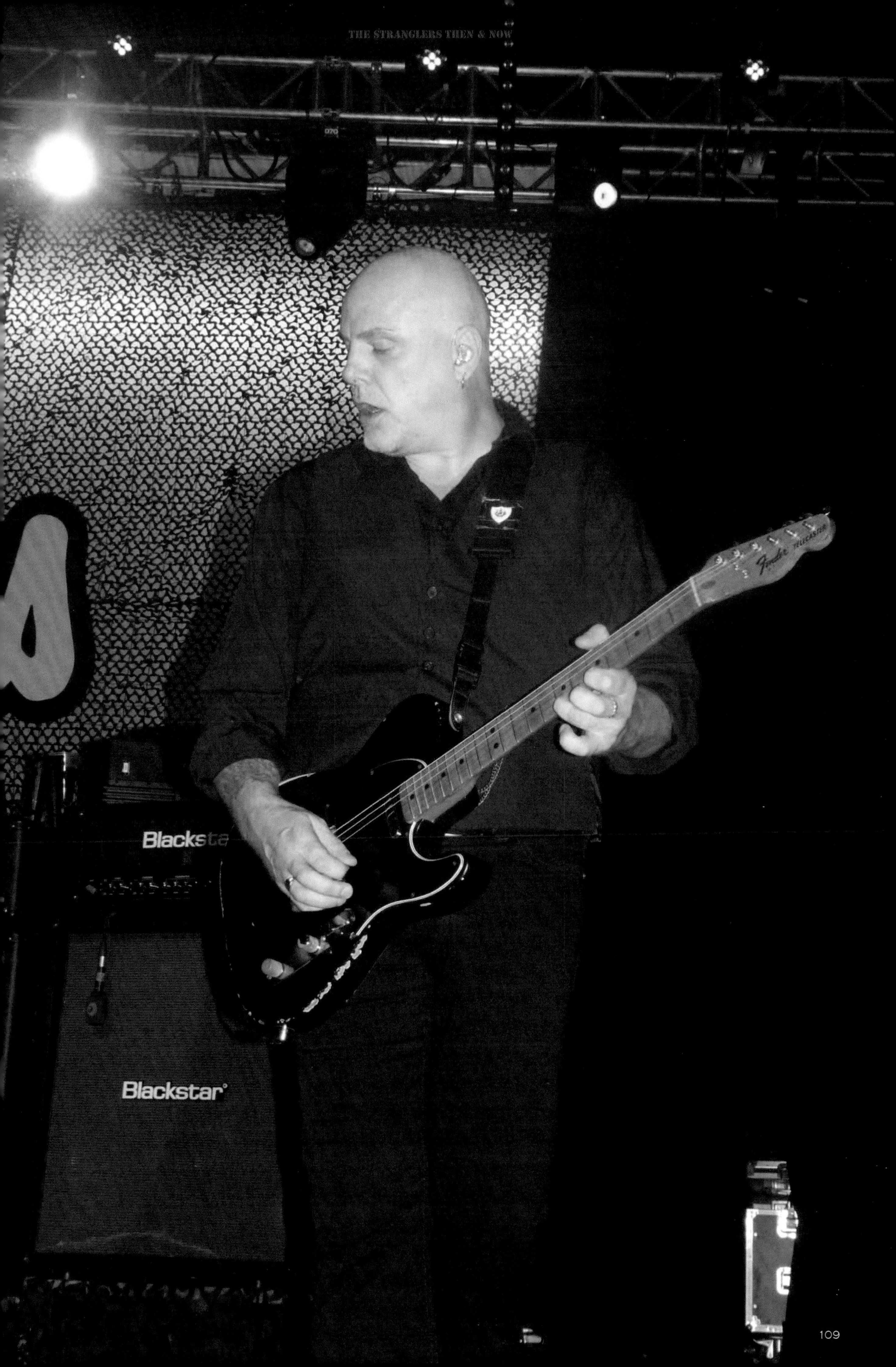
Blackstar
Blackstar
Fender TELECASTER

"It's hard to keep up with some of the older stuff, but you've got to do what you've got to do. After 40 years, it's like driving a car. I enjoy the fun without thinking about it. I can't recall the last time it felt a chore. This is the best band in the world — and we'll carry on 'til we can't any more. Though we are not thinking about that!"
Jet Black, Oxford Times, March 2014

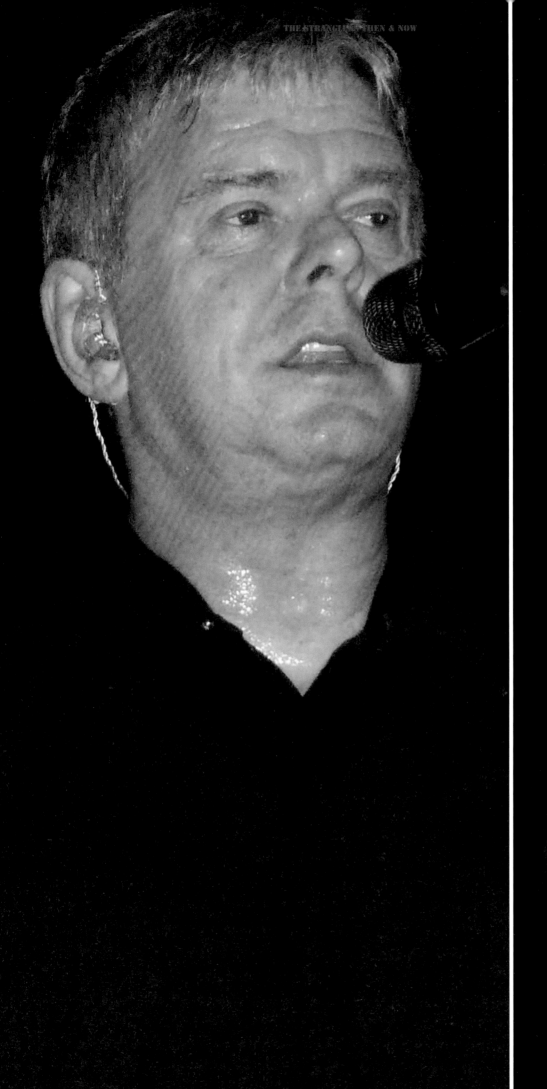

"With the best will in the world everybody gets older. Your stamina and strength goes, and it's difficult to keep up with a band like we are. It takes a lot of energy. Jet hasn't travelled abroad with us for a while when we were doing shows in the US, Australia and Japan. I spoke to Jet half-an-hour ago, he gives us all his fond good wishes, but he would rather The Stranglers progress without him than not be at all. His leaving has been a gradual process — inspirationally he will always be a touchstone and totem for us. Whenever he can make an appearance he will."
Baz Warne, The Argus, 10th July 2015

"I start one hour before stage time with fifteen minutes of squeezing Play Dough. This helps wake up all the muscles in the forearms. After that I move on to five minutes of stretching my fingers, wrists, and hands. Then I get changed and rub my hands with surgical spirit. A climber friend of mine gave me that tip and it's amazing for avoiding blister. Thirty minutes from stage time and the excitement is building! Time for a bottle of water and a Berocca! Then it's fifteen minutes on a practice pad, another water and a banana, then fifteen more minutes on the pad, and BOOM! Gig time! I do these things religiously and not only do they help me play well but they also help me get my mind focused to perform at my best."
Jim Macaulay, Modern Drummer, 2017

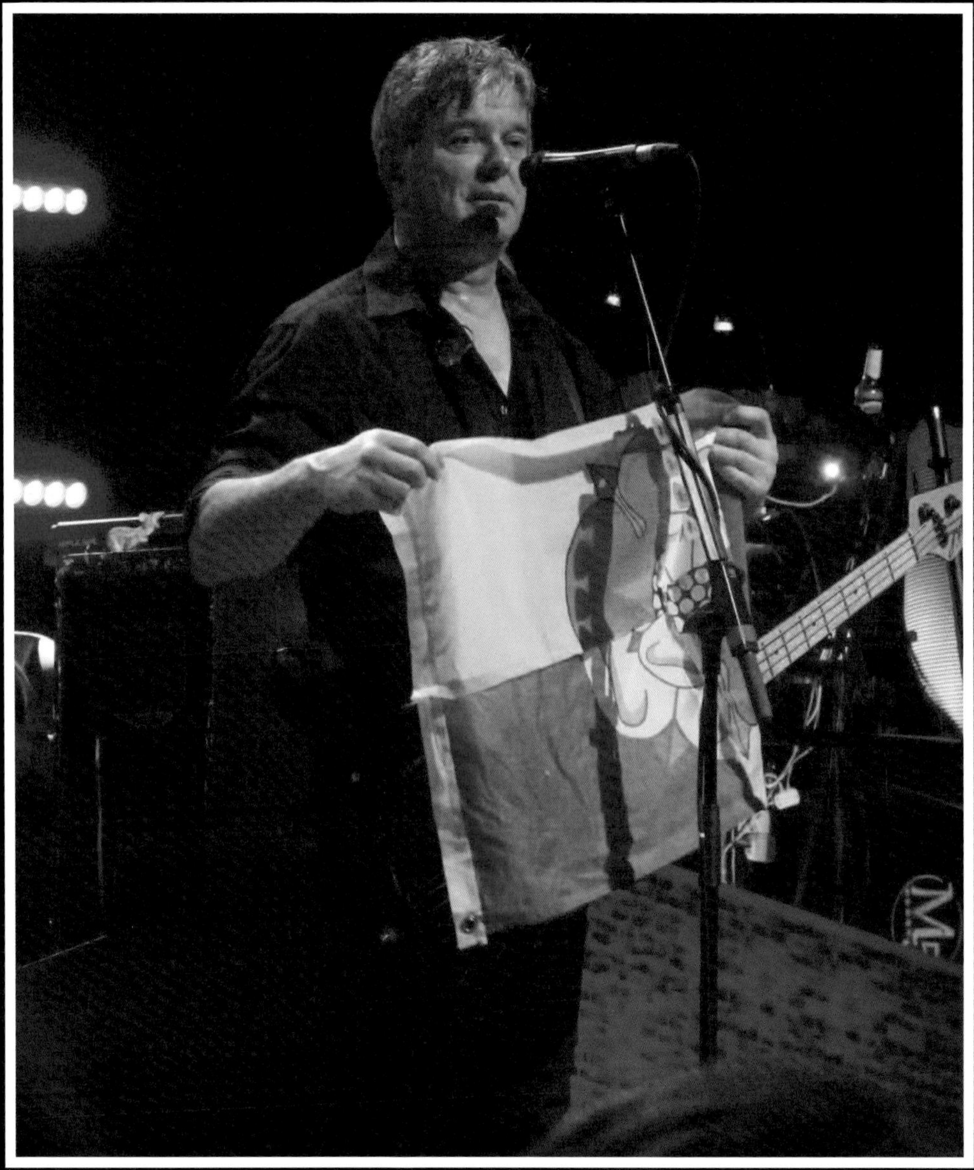

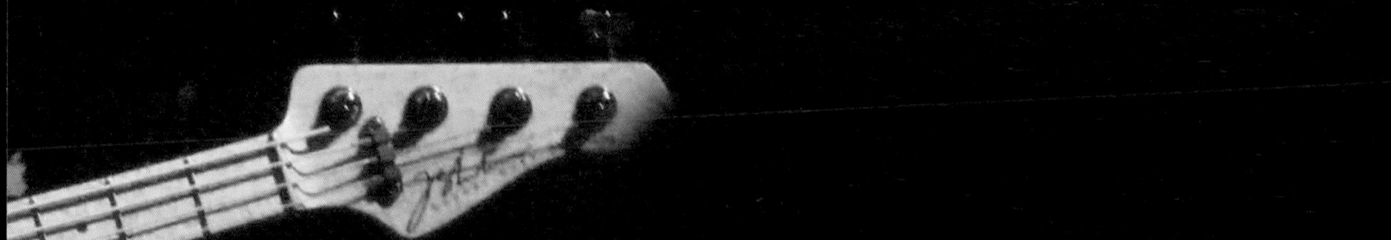

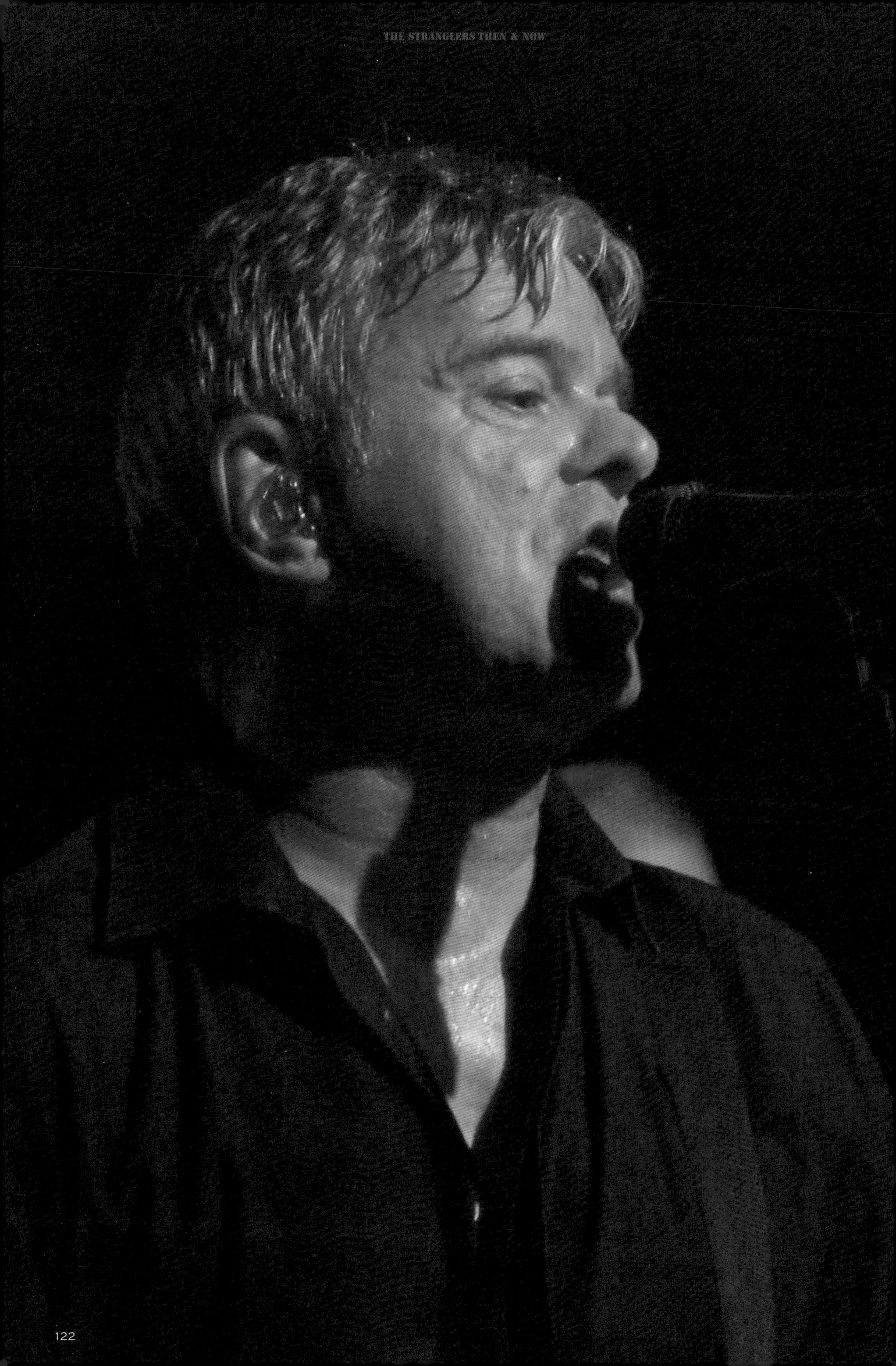

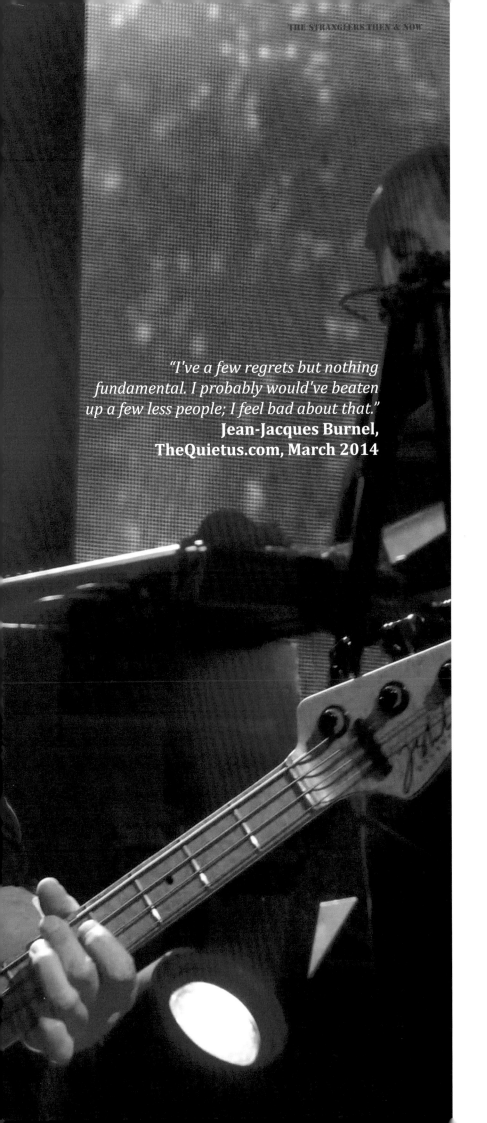

"I've a few regrets but nothing fundamental. I probably would've beaten up a few less people; I feel bad about that."
**Jean-Jacques Burnel,
TheQuietus.com, March 2014**

DEDICATED IN BLACK

"We have just lost a dear friend and music genius, and so has the whole world. Dave was a complete natural in music. Together, we toured the globe endlessly and it was clear he was adored by millions. A huge talent, a great loss, he is dearly missed."
Jet Black

"We stood together on the same side of the stage for 20 years, laughed, joked and shared our lives in the way that only band mates can. I'll miss him forever."
Baz Warne

"He just didn't have the filters that 'normal' people have. A lot of people don't and that's what gives them their savant, their genius. They can't get distracted."
Jean-Jacques Burnel

"He was the difference between the Stranglers and every other punk band. His musical skill and gentle nature gave an interesting twist to the band. He should be remembered as the man who gave the world the music of Golden Brown."
Hugh Cornwell

We duly acknowledge the following people who all put their faith in this publication by pre-ordering it:

Gary Abbott
Simon Austin
Natalie Banks
Steve Bell
Helen Bennett
Andrew Bishop
Douglas Bradford
Paul Davies
Colin Davis
James Dorman
Norman Emmerson
Richard Evans
Robert Fairlie
Deborah Field

James Fisher
Tam Getty
Paul Gibson
Neil Glass
Julian Hight
Scott Hornby
Victoria Jackson
Karen Lowe
Robert Magee
Iain McIntosh
Alan McNiven
Steve Milne
Rosemarie Milner
Andy Mitchell

Mark Oliff
Sharon Parfitt
Graham Pearce
Chris Price
Kevin Rankin
Mike Riley
Joe Salmon
Ian Snaith
Colin Wade
Amanda Watson
Bob White
Chris Wilkins
Paul Woodcock
Stephen Wright

PHOTO CREDITS

Steve Emberton: Wardour Street, Soho, London, 1976 - p8, 10, 11-12; Hammersmith Odeon, London, October 1976 - p14-18. All other images are by Alan Perry and were taken at the following venues: Locarno Ballroom, Coventry, 4th October 1977 - p20-27; Battersea Park, London, 16th September 1978 - p28-53; Wembley Stadium, London, 18th August 1979 - p54-59; Coventry Theatre, Coventry, 4th March 1981 - p60-69; Reading Festival, 27th August 1983 - p70-73; Robin 2, Bilston, 30th June 2006 - p76-83. The rest of the images were all taken at the O2 Academy, Birmingham as follows: 13th March 2010 - p84-99; 19th March 2011 - p100-103; 16th March 2013 - p104-107; 14th March 2015 - p108-111; 12th March 2016 - p112-117; 18th March 2017 - p118-123; 17th March 2018 - p124-127.